Beyond The Words

Rhythms of the heart

Savita Kumari

BookLeaf Publishing

India | USA | UK

Made with ❤ on the BookLeaf Publishing Platform
www.bookleafpub.in
www.bookleafpub.com

Dedication

"To the dreamers, the lovers, and the guardians of
compassion,
Who see the world with eyes of empathy and kindness,
Who nurture the beauty of nature, and cherish the lives
of all beings,
This book is dedicated to you, the beacons of hope.

May our collective dreams, and shared humanity,
Inspire a world where love, compassion, and empathy
thrive.
May our words be a testament to the power of kindness,
And may our hearts continue to beat with the rhythm of
love.

To the pure souls who care, who give, and who uplift,
Your love and compassion are the lifeblood of humanity.
May this book be a reflection of the beauty you bring,
And may it inspire others to join you on this journey of
love and kindness."

Preface

"As I poured my heart into these poems, I aimed to capture the essence of human experience across generations. From the innocence of childhood to the turbulence of adolescence, the passion of youth, and the wisdom of middle age, I've sought to express the complexities of life's journey.

Through my words, I've tried to offer guidance for parents navigating the challenges of raising children in today's world. I've woven in parenting tips and cyber safety advice, hoping to empower contemporary parents with the tools they need to support their children's growth.

But beyond guidance, my ultimate desire is to spread happiness and love. I believe that poetry has the power to touch hearts, to heal, and to inspire. My hope is that these pocms will resonate with readers of all ages, offering solace, comfort, and joy.

In a world that often seems divided, I dream of a future where love, kindness, and compassion reign supreme. I envision a world where children grow up with confidence and curiosity, where adolescents find their voice and purpose, and where adults live with wisdom and fulfillment.

If these poems can inspire even a single person to spread love and happiness, then I will consider my efforts worthwhile. I offer these words as a gift to humanity, with the hope that they will find a place in your heart and inspire you to make a positive impact in the world.

Acknowledgements

"I extend my deepest gratitude to my loving husband, whose unwavering support and guidance have been my rock throughout this journey. To my extraordinary children, you are my boundless source of inspiration, motivation, and positivity. Your sparkling eyes, curious minds, and joyful spirits ignite a fire within me, pushing me to explore, create, and grow.

Your appreciation and enthusiasm are the greatest rewards, filling my heart with happiness and encouraging me to strive for more. This book is a testament to the love, energy, and inspiration you've shared with me. I'm forever grateful to have you all in my life."

1. Eternal Embrace

"My love for you, a flame that burns so bright,
Even in death's dark veil, my arms will hold you tight.
If paradise were mine, I'd surrender its gate,
And trade eternal bliss for just one moment's fate,
To be with you, my love, my guiding star,
My heart beats for you, near and far.

The world may change, its seasons come and go,
New melodies may rise, but our love will forever glow.
A hundred excuses may try to erase our past,
But reality stands firm, a love that will forever last.
Through life's darkest night, your love shines like a light,
A beacon in the storm, my guiding sight.

If fate were cruel, and ripped you from my side,
My love would not falter, it would be my heart's pride.
The thought of moonbeams dancing on your skin,
Is a beauty I'd claim, my love within.
Even divine hands, that shape the universe's design,
Would stir my envy, if they dared to touch your divine.

My love for you, a fortress strong and true,
Even in death's cold grasp, my heart will hold you anew.
In every lifetime, in every realm, in every dream,
My love for you will echo, a love supreme."

2. Unveiling Womanhood

We rise with a chorus of voices entwined,
In the tapestry of history, our legacy defined.
With courage stitched within every seam,
We forge the future, igniting each dream.

In shadows we gather, a sisterhood's might,
Bound by the stories that flicker and ignite.
Our journeys relentless, we carry the spark,
Guiding the lost through the cold, daunting dark.

As rivers flow fiercely, so does our soul,
In the heart of our struggles, we find our whole.
Together we flourish, with roots running deep,
In the fertile soil where our hopes gently seep.

With each whispered promise, a world we will build,
Where every woman rises, every heart is filled.
In unity's strength, we shatter the chains,
And dance to the rhythm of freedom's refrains.

Through valleys of hardship, through mountains of fear,
Each step is a triumph, our vision made clear.
With laughter like sunshine and tears that have healed,
We weave a new fabric, our destinies sealed.

For every voice silenced, a thousand will sing,
In the cadence of courage, our spirits take wing.
Together we're woven, a powerful strand,
In the fabric of fortune, we'll firmly stand.

3. Dreams Beyond Bounds

From childhood I have seen many dreams
and believed they would become true
And with faith in my heart I have held on to
them, through and through
Just as a ship needs a harbor to steer,
Dreams give life its directions and purpose clear
I have set sail on life's journey with dreams
as my guide,
Trusting they will navigate me through life's
ebb and tide
Some dreams reached their promised
land, others fell by side
But wisdom and experience bloomed
With each step I took with pride
Dreams know no wealth no social divide
Every soul has hopes every heart has a stride
The weary laborer a poor child the brick-carrier too
All dreams of better tomorrows with aspiration true
I have learned to dream without limits no strings to hold
Dream big aim high and you will reach heights to behold

For even in shadows, where doubts may grow,
A flicker of courage ignites the glow,
With every heartbeat, a rhythm to chase,
In the tapestry of life, dreams weave their grace.
So I will cherish each vision, each whispering thought,
For in the garden of dreaming, resilience is wrought.
Let the stars be my witness, let the winds be my song,
In this symphony of hope, together we belong.

4. The Seeds of Joy

Happiness is a dance, improvising in time,
With each step we take, to the rhythm sublime.
It revels in laughter, in whispers of trust,
In moments we cherish, in the small and the just.
Like stars that twinkle in the velvet sky,
Happiness is a wish upon which we rely.

So nurture your garden, let your spirit bloom,
With seeds of compassion that conquer the gloom.
Let gratitude sing in a chorus so true,
For the more that we offer, the more comes to you.
Joy is a lantern that guides through the night,
Illuminating paths where love feels so right.

Hold fast to your dreams, let their colors unfurl,
In the grand symphony of this wondrous world.
For happiness flows from the heart that gives free,
A melody timeless, our shared legacy.

5. Love's Gentle Breeze

"In fortune's gentle breeze, I found my way,

With you, my guiding star, on life's journey's day.

Time's fleeting moments, like autumn leaves, did stray,

Yet, in your eyes, my heart found a gentle way.

My flaws, a canvas, of imperfections worn,

Like moonlit shadows, on a midnight morn.

But your acceptance, a warm, golden light,

Illuminated my path, and banished endless night.

With you, I learned to flow, like a river's gentle stream,

Calming my storms, and soothing my troubled dream.

Your presence, a shelter, from life's raging sea,

A haven where love, and peace, dwell in harmony.

In life's garden, we've walked, hand in hand,

Through thorns of sorrow, and roses of love's command.

We've danced beneath starry skies, and weathered life's
storms,

Together, our love, a flame, that burns, and forever
forms.

Trials and tribulations, like tempests, raged and roared,

But our love, a beacon, shone bright, and forever soared.

We've laughed, we've cried, we've lived, and loved, and
grown,

Through every moment, our bond, has forever been
sown.

Like water and salt, we've merged, as one,

Our love, a blend, of hearts, forever won.

In your arms, I've found, a peaceful nest,

A love that's pure, and true, and forever at its best.

With every breath, I'll cherish our past,

And look forward, to our future, that will forever last.

Our love, a masterpiece, of moments, shared and true,

A bond that's strong, and forever shines through.

6. The Art of Living

"I'm learning to see, beyond the facade,

To watch and wait, and not be swayed.

I'm learning to let go, of expectations high,

To find joy in surprises, and a gentle sigh.

Life's a journey, forward we stride,

Ups and downs, we'll weather with pride.

I'm learning to understand, the emptiness within,

The longing for happiness, that many can't win.

Their unhappiness, a reflection of their pain,

Jealousy and envy, a cycle in vain.

I'm learning to respond, with calm and gentle might,

To neutralize the negativity, and shine with inner light.

I'll wear a smile, despite the criticism's sting,

And maintain my empathy, my heart's gentle wing.

I'm learning to let go, of the need to please,

For it's impossible, to bring joy to all, if you squeeze.

Not every question, demands an answer true,

Not every challenge, requires a response anew.

Sometimes silence speaks, louder than words can say,

And in stillness, we find our own way.

If something drains, your positivity's might,

Let it go, and walk away, into the light.

I'll cherish those, who've loved me true,

And stood by me, through life's joys and pursuits anew.

I'll live life fully, with a heart full of cheer,

And hum a gentle tune, despite life's uncertainty here.

7. The Parenting Guide

In today's world, parenting's a test,

With depression, anxiety, and peer pressure's unrest.

Social media's maze, a challenge to face,

We must guide our children, with a gentle, loving pace.

Let's motivate them to be confident and bright,

By exploring their creativity, and shining with delight.

Prepare their bags, and take responsibility's call,

No blaming others, just learn and stand tall.

Happiness comes from within, don't you know?

A smile's a reward, that glows and grows.

Let's create happy hours, with laughter and glee,

No fights, no complaints, just joyful moments to be.

Integrity's the key, to a heart that's true,

A cordial environment, where feelings shine through.

Respect and politeness, a gentle way to be,

We'll teach our children, to live with integrity.

Independence is key, to growth and might,

Let's allow them to choose, and make decisions bright.

Respect their achievements, and let them take the lead,

Their friends and choices, we'll support with love and
speed.

Hard work and diligence, a path to success,

Let's encourage exploration, and a love to express.

Their room's their responsibility, to keep it tidy and
clean,

A lesson in ownership, and a habit serene.

Sensitivity's a gift, that touches hearts so dear,

Let's teach our children, to be kind and always near.

No fighting in front, just love and gentle care,

We'll nurture their emotions, with a sensitive air.

Love and appreciation, a bond that's strong and true,

A hug goodbye, and a listening ear, that's what we'll do.

Small achievements matter, let's celebrate with glee,

Appreciate their friends, and the love they bring to see.

Environmental awareness, a lesson so grand,

Let's guide them to nature, and the beauty of the land.

Conserve water and light, and live with care,

A sustainable future, we'll help them prepare.

With love, patience, and guidance, we'll lead the way,

Our children will thrive, in a brighter day.

Let's nurture their hearts, and minds so bright,

And help them grow, into compassionate, confident light.

8. The Digital Dilemma

"In this digital haze, where screens reign supreme,

We've lost the touch, of life's vibrant dream.

Children's laughter echoes, in virtual space,

As gadgets replace, the joy of a warm, human face.

Their tiny hands, once held crayons bright,

Now clutch smartphones, in a digital light.

Alexa's voice, a distant hum, replaces mother's tone,

Poems on TV, a hollow sound, as humanity's lost, alone.

In rooms filled with people, we're alone, you see,

Each face aglow, in social media's virtual sea.

We crave connection, yet we're lost in the crowd,

Our relationships reduced, to online, empty avow.

Creativity's spark, fades away, it's true,

As one-touch answers, stifle minds anew.

Children's imagination, once a soaring flight,

Now confined, to screens' limited light.

Their social skills, wither away, unseen,

As virtual friends, replace real ones, a digital sheen.

Their cyber safety, a ticking bomb, unseen,

Social identity, hacked, their future's sheen.

The danger's real, the threat's so grand,

Life and future, hanging in the balance, hand in hand.

Let's beware, of screens' sly might,

Reduce screen time, and take flight.

Let's reconnect, with life's vibrant hue,

With nature's beauty, and love that's true.

Let's nurture minds, that think and explore,

And guide our children, to a world beyond the screen's score."

9. Nature's Guidance

"Nature's wisdom, a lesson every day,

A tranquil lake, teaches us to stay.

Unfazed by turmoil, like stones thrown in,

It keeps its essence, calm and serene within.

The sun's radiance, a beacon bright,

Inspires us to shine, despite the darkest night.

With warmth and light, it dispels the gloom,

Illuminating paths, to banish doubt and gloom.

The mountain's steadfastness, a lesson true,

Teaches us to stand firm, amidst life's stormy brew.

Unshaken and strong, it weathers every test,

A symbol of resilience, forever at its best.

Colorful flowers, a gentle breeze,

Remind us to spread joy, with every step we seize.

Their fragrance and beauty, a gift to share,

Enriching lives, with love and care.

The creeper's embrace, a symbol of love,

Teaches us to welcome, sent from above.

With open arms, we hug the world tight,

Spreading warmth, and making everything right.

The shade's cool comfort, a peaceful sight,

Inspires us to soothe, and calm the night.

By giving solace, we ease the pain,

And bring tranquility, like a summer rain.

Like a flowing river, we must keep moving ahead,

Creating our path, with every step we've tread.

If we keep our minds closed, and hearts confined,

How will we find joy, or let love in?

The world reflects, what we hold within,

Darkness or light, the choice is ours to win.

Those who light the lamp, of knowledge and love,

Illuminate the world, sent from above.

10. The Frantic Pace

"Life's canvas, a blur of frantic hue,

Each face, a story, of dreams anew.

The city roars, a cacophony of sound,

As souls rush by, with hearts unbound.

In this whirlwind, we search for peace,

A fleeting dream, that our souls release.

We've lost our way, in life's endless grind,

And forgotten joy, left far behind.

The morning rush, a chaotic sight,

Strangers passing, without a gentle light.

The father's gaze, on tomorrow's test,

The mother's care, for her child's rest.

The student's haste, to reach the classroom door,

The vendor's cry, amidst the city's roar.

Each step a stride, in life's mad dance,

A frantic pace, that takes its chance.

The weight of life, a burden we bear,

A heart that's heavy, with no time to share.

We're balloons, inflated, ready to burst,

Our emotions raw, our hearts, a fragile first.

In this chaos, we lose ourselves, it's true,

And struggle to find, our hearts anew.

The world outside, a maze to navigate,

A life of fragments, forever to create.

Yet, in the stillness, we find our voice,

A whispered truth, that makes some noise.

A chance to breathe, to let go our fears,

To find our hearts, and calm our tears.

11. Drizzle of Feelings

"Today, emotions drizzled, like a gentle hue,

Calming the heart, with a soothing dew.

The outside rain, a calming melody,

Quenched the thirst of my soul, like a summer's symphony.

On this wet earth, tender shoots appear,

New and old feelings, like flowers, bloom here.

The petrichor scent, a perfume so sweet,

Stirred memories, like a storm, at our feet.

Leaning on your shoulder, heart's garden thrives,

Nature's rhythm, a love that survives.

The trees, like sentinels, stood tall and still,

Their leaves, a gentle rustle, a soothing thrill.

The rain's gentle touch, a balm to the skin,

Washed away worries, like dust, within.

Ginger and cardamom tea, a warm delight,

Comforted the heart, in morning's golden light.

This whimsical weather, though fleeting, true,

Awakened heartstrings, a new melody anew.

In the heart's strings, a new harmony was born,

A symphony, that will echo, till the next rain's form.

Life's rhythm, now in tune, will softly sway,

Awaiting the next shower, to dance another day.

For in the rain's refrain, we find our peace,

A calming solace, that our souls release."

12. Hope's Gentle Light

"Hope's gentle hand, a lifeline true,

Faith's thread, forever shining through.

Life's turbulent seas, may toss us around,

When anchors fail, and shores are lost, profound.

Yet hope's steady oar, guides us through the night,

A beacon in darkness, shining with all its might.

It whispers softly, "Hold on, don't let go,"

A reassuring voice, that helps us navigate life's flow.

When sorrow's dark clouds, gather in the sky,

Hope's sunbeams pierce, and light the way, to a brighter high.

The heart may ache, but hope's warmth remains,

A comforting presence, that soothes life's pains.

Fate's bouquet, holds thorns alongside roses fair,

While petals fragrance life, thorns bring pain we can't share.

But hope's voice whispers, petals may fade,

Yet thorns, like resilience, forever displayed.

For every step forward, we take with fear,

Hope's gentle nudge, encourages us to persevere.

It reminds us that, even in darkest night,

There's always a glimmer, of morning light.

Embracing hope, and pushing despair away,

Brings peace and joy, to brighten each new day.

Those who learn to smile, through life's darkest test,

Have won the battle, and hope's promise, forever blessed.

13. Humanity Lost

"Where does this darkness stem from, I wonder?

Why do humans spread such terror, such thunder?

Is it innate, or learned from birth?

Do parents sow seeds of hate, on this earth?

Who hands them guns, who poisons their mind?

Who turns them from human to beast, so unkind?

Why don't their hands tremble, as they take a life?

Why doesn't their soul protest, in endless strife?

Why don't their fingers quiver, as they touch and defile?

Why don't they recoil, at blood's crimson trial?

This brutality transcends, all creed and all faith,

These individuals, bound by no moral wraith.

They see their kin's blood, as sacred and dear,

Yet others' lives, mere water, without a tear.

They mourn their own losses, with anguished cry,

Yet find joy in killing, with a twisted sigh.

Their own family's honor, they hold so high,

Yet others' dignity, they trample, without a sigh.

Beasts hunt for survival, with instinctual might,

But humans, the greatest beasts, kill without a fight."

14. Whispers of Youth

"Childhood's laughter echoes, fading away,

Adolescence unfurls, with youthful sway.

Toys and games, once delightful, now lose their charm,

Eyes that once sparkled, now whisper secrets, disarm.

The world, a canvas, transforms with every gaze,

Perspectives shift, like shifting sands' daze.

Self-discovery dawns, with mirror's gentle might,

Reflecting dreams, and desires, in morning light.

Romeo and Juliet's tale, Heer-Ranjha's love so true,

Captivate the heart, with emotions, pure and new.

Some crave conversation, others solitude's peace,

Some seek identity, while questions swirl, release.

Career aspirations rise, like morning sun's rays,

Love's tender flame, ignites, in secret ways.

Dreams unfold, like petals of a flower,

With vibrant colors, life's canvas, hour by hour.

Nature's beauty beckons, like a gentle stream,

Heart weaves new designs, in life's intricate dream.

Dreams burst with colors, like rainbows' vibrant lines,

Life's possibilities, endless, like an open shrine.

Parental guidance fades, friends' words resonate,

A phase of life, emotions surge, dreams create.

This youthful stage, a time of emotional tide,

Best phase of life, where dreams and passion reside.

If you're navigating this age, savor every delight,

For it flees like wind, never to return in sight.

Immerse in colors, paint life's canvas wide,

Make your life a rainbow, let youthful spirit glide."

15. Radiance of Savita

My parents bestowed upon me a name that predestined
my path,

Savita, meaning sun, a radiant beam that shines so
bright.

Derived from Sanskrit, it embodies the sun's virtues too,

Illumination, inspiration, and life's purpose, a guiding
light that shines through.

As a teacher, I've lit the way for countless students'
futures bright,

Embodying the essence of Savita, a ray of hope in
darkness and night.

My personality, a blend of warmth and light,

Has touched lives, though sometimes its intensity has
ignited friction's spark in sight.

Through life's trials, I've kept my inner fire burning
strong,

A flame that flickers, yet never goes wrong.

Though hidden, my heart beats with compassion and
love,

Yearning to illuminate souls, sent from above.

I've forged my own path, lived life on my terms,

Success born from hard work, not just fate's whims.

My name's significance resonates deep within me,

A constant reminder of purpose, a spark that sets me
free."

16. Aging Gracefully

Time slips away like sand, lines etch on my face,

Gray hair whispers farewell to youth's fleeting pace.

Yet, this foolish heart resists, unaware of time's flow,

A river's current, taking us where we don't know.

The world once shone bright, now sometimes seems dull,

A phase of life where magic faded, reality's pull.

When young, my heart was alive, full of zest and cheer,

But life's journey taught me sorrow, and doubts creep near.

Change is life's constant, maturity brings stability,

Though childhood's laughter and youth's poetry still resonate with me.

Solitude brings peace, yet memories of joy remain,

A bittersweet reminder of life's transient refrain.

As I age, I've learned to embrace the flow,

To find strength in vulnerability, and let my spirit glow.

Though time may take its toll, my eyes still sparkle bright,

Dreams and desires remain, a flame that burns with all its might.

Oh, my Lord, grant me this wish: may my heart stay young,

May desires and passions remain, till my life's final song.

For a youthful spirit is life's greatest wealth, indeed,

A treasure that transcends time, and brings true peace
and creed.

Youth's farewell, but not to my heart's relentless beat,

For every ending carries hope, in shadows, light we
greet.

Each wrinkle tells a story, each gray a lesson learned,

A tapestry of moments lived, in love and wisdom earned.

So as I watch the sunset fade, I see the stars arise,

In every dusk, a promise, a chance to realize—

That though the years may whisper soft of what I leave
behind,

My spirit dances on the breeze, forever intertwined.

17. Immeasurable Pain

"Who can measure the depths of sorrow?

Can it be quantified, compared, or ranked?

Whose pain is greater, whose is less?

Who can truly tell?

The farmer, worn by crop failures' weight,

The coal miner, facing death's daily fate,

The daily wage worker, grieving lost work's might,

The factory worker, laid off, without a fight.

The mother, rationing meager food for her kin,

The laborer, hiding tattered clothes within,

The father, struggling to gather dowry's toll,

Parents, anguished by children's jobless role.

The youth, entangled in addiction's snare,

The sex worker, enduring physical, mental pain to share,

The child, subjected to abuse, a tender age's scar,

The father, carrying his child's bier, tears afar.

The mother, shielding her daughter's tarnished name,

Each story, a testament to suffering's endless claim."

"Who can measure the depths of sorrow?

...

Each story, a testament to suffering's endless claim.

Yet, amidst the pain, a glimmer shines,

A resilience that weaves, a hope that binds.

For in the darkness, hearts still beat,

And in the silence, whispers of kindness meet.

In this sea of suffering, we're not alone,

Our shared humanity, a bridge to call home.

Let's hold each other, through the darkest night,

And find solace, in the warmth of human light."

18. Elusive Mind

"The flickering mind, a bird on wing,

Defies all bounds, its freedom clings.

A whimsical wanderer, seeking skies unknown,

A gentle breeze that whispers secrets, unconfined.

Like a lost child, it strays, and must be found,

Tethered by threads of mindfulness, gently bound.

Yet, like a river's flow, it bursts its banks,

A fragile glass wall, shattered by life's turbulent tanks.

The mind, a kite on strings of thought,

Dances on winds of joy, or sorrow caught.

When strings are cut, it soars, a fleeting dream,

Lost in the vast expanse, its path unseen.

But minds can meet, like scents that blend,

In harmony, their essence transcends.

They dance with joy, exuberant and free,

A symphony of connection, wild and carefree.

A delicate balance, the mind maintains,

Between light and darkness, its fragile refrains.

Stained by shadows, it yearns to break free,

Mindfulness whispers solace, a gentle reprieve."

19. Echoes of Memories

Time trickles like clock, memories the only remains,

A pang in the heart, shadows on water, ephemeral pains.

We forget words spoken, but memories close to heart,

Return like rain, flooding us with joy, laughter, and every part.

Our foolish heart calls out, though time won't turn back,

Memories fragrant like damp earth, dry roses, and love's tender track.

The ache transforms to tears, a testament to our pain,

A poignant reminder of love's beauty and heart's refrain.

In moments of solitude, those memories resurface,

Like whispers of the past, a bittersweet, nostalgic verse.

The scent of wet earth rises, transporting us back,

To laughter, tears, and moments that forever leave their
mark.

Though time moves on, memories stay, a treasured past,

A legacy of love, forever etched within our hearts at last.

The heart, though battered, still holds on to what's dear,

A testament to love's enduring power, despite the
passing year.

As twilight descends, we gather fragments of light,

In the tapestry of time, where shadows dance in flight.

With every heartbeat, echoes of joy, a sweet refrain,

We carry the weight of love, like blossoms after rain.

20. A Walk Down Memory Lane

Today, memories grasped my hand once more,

Leading me through familiar, nostalgic streets.

She's a playful companion, arriving unannounced,

Oblivious to time, a whimsical guest.

She shows me old dreams, shared with friends so dear,

College days, laughter, and memories so clear.

The old building, college fests, new dresses to wear,

Waiting hours at bus stops, without a care.

Chemistry lab, lecturers' scolding tone,

Getting kicked out of class, yet laughter overthrown.

We'd sneak in, mask off, to watch Dilwale Dulhania,

Enduring three-day suspensions, a memory to cherish.

Boys would praise, Bollywood songs would play,

We'd fib about our names, and giggle all day.

These memories whirl me around, lost in time,

Streets of yesteryear, a nostalgic rhyme.

If not for my mom's voice, calling from behind,

"Where are you? Why aren't you talking? What's on
your mind?"

I'd be lost in thoughts, a smile my only reply,

A pang in my heart, a nostalgic sigh

21. Free to Laugh

"Childhood's laughter echoes, a melodic refrain,

Like morning temple bells, their joyous chime and strain.

The gentle gurgle of a river's flow, crystal clear,

Reflects the purity of heart, untouched by fear.

Soft as velvet's touch, the tender dew-kissed petals sway,

Like anklets' rhythmic tinkling, dancing through the day.

The flute's sweet, soothing melody, a symphony divine,

Can thaw the frost of sorrow, and make the heart
entwine.

Oh, to laugh with abandon, unencumbered and free,

Shedding life's formalities, embracing pure glee.

Like a masterpiece of art, childhood's joy, so pure and
bright,

Can melt the stoniest of hearts, and bring forth delight.

May we recapture that innocence, that carefree grin,

And let our laughter flow, like a river's waters within.

For in the simplicity of childhood's joy, we find,

A treasure trove of happiness, forever to bind